D1369303

DEFINING EVENTS
of the Twenty-First Century

CATASTROPHES
in the Twenty-First Century

by Carolyn Williams-Noren

ReferencePoint
Press®

San Diego, CA

For more information, contact:
ReferencePoint Press, Inc.
PO Box 27779
San Diego, CA 92198
www.ReferencePointPress.com

LIBRARY OF CONGRESS CATALOGING-IN-PUBLICATION DATA

Names: Williams-Noren, Carolyn, author.
Title: Catastrophes in the twenty-first century / by Carolyn Williams-Noren.
Other titles: Catastrophes in the 21st century
Description: San Diego, CA : ReferencePoint Press, Inc., [2020] | Series:
    Defining Events of the Twenty-First Century | Audience: Grades: 9 to 12. |
    Includes bibliographical references and index.
Identifiers: LCCN 2019000779 (print) | LCCN 2019010596 (ebook) | ISBN
    9781682826034 (ebook) | ISBN 9781682826010 (hardcover)
Subjects: LCSH: Natural disasters--Juvenile literature. | Environmental
    disasters--Juvenile literature.
Classification: LCC GB5019 (ebook) | LCC GB5019 .W55 2020 (print) | DDC
    303.48/5--dc23
LC record available at https://lccn.loc.gov/2019000779

CONTENTS

IMPORTANT EVENTS

2011
In March, a 9.0 magnitude earthquake, severe tsunami, and nuclear meltdown slam northeastern Japan.

2014
Flint, Michigan, changes its water source and treatment system, beginning a series of events that exposes residents to high lead levels and other contaminants for many months.

2010
A 7.0 magnitude earthquake strikes Haiti on January 12. It leaves 316,000 people dead and 1.5 million without shelter.

2014
The largest-ever outbreak of Ebola sickens and kills tens of thousands of people in Guinea, Sierra Leone, Liberia, and beyond.

2005   2010   2015

2010
On April 20, a blowout on the Deepwater Horizon offshore oil rig causes huge explosions and eleven casualties.

2015
Indonesia's worst wildfire season on record burns vast swaths of forest and farmland and blankets southeast Asia with a sickening haze.

2017
Following years of escalating persecution, the Myanmar military brutally attacks members of the Rohingya ethnic group and burns hundreds of Rohingya villages.

2018
Brazil's 200-year-old National Museum goes up in flames on September 2.

2017
In August, Hurricane Harvey floods the Texas coast in the most intense hurricane rainfall ever recorded in the United States.

2017
In June, President Donald Trump announces his intention to withdraw from the Paris climate agreement.

2015

2020

2015
Meeting in Paris in December, representatives of 195 countries including the United States reach an agreement to lower greenhouse gas emissions in order to slow global warming.

2018
In September, a nonprofit launches a cleanup system to gather and remove floating trash from the Great Pacific Garbage Patch.

Rising Waters in Houston

People in Houston, on Texas's Gulf Coast, expect hurricanes. On average, a hurricane strikes there every nine to sixteen years. So preparing for high winds, blackouts, and rain is part of life. For days before a storm strikes, people secure plywood to protect windows, stockpile provisions, and get ready for days spent indoors, potentially without electricity.

In August 2017, the Houston area took a wallop from the strongest hurricane to hit the United States since Hurricane Katrina in 2005. The storm, given the name Hurricane Harvey, gained speed quickly as it approached the coast. Its winds created a storm surge, bringing coastal waters 10 feet (3 m) above ground level and flooding the coastline.

The rain exceeded everyone's expectations. The storm stalled over Houston, pouring rain on the city. So much rain fell that the National Weather Service had to add new colors to its rainfall maps. In two days, parts of Houston got as much rain as they typically receive in a whole year: 51 inches (130 cm). Combined, the rain and storm surge caused catastrophic flooding. The National Hurricane Center

The floodwaters brought by Hurricane Harvey's waves and rainfall devastated much of Houston. Whole neighborhoods were drenched in feet of water.

called it "the most significant tropical cyclone rainfall event in United States history."[1]

At the home of Maya Wadler, age seventeen, the water "bubbled up from the doors, seeped in from the windows." She said, "Everywhere you turned, there would just be a new flowing puddle. It just kept filling. . . . I was so scared. We didn't know what would happen. And there is no one you can call." Eventually, her family was able to ride to safety in a dump truck driven by rescue workers.[2]

Wadler's was one of more than 204,000 homes in the Houston area damaged or destroyed by Harvey. The floodwaters soaked belongings and structures, generating over 13 million cubic yards (10 million cubic m) of debris. And fifty people died in Houston, most of them by drowning.

Long-Term Impact

The destruction didn't stop when the storm rolled out. A recently flooded area isn't just wet. It's full of contaminants, unwanted wildlife, and, later, mold and potentially disease-carrying mosquitoes. The area's oil refineries and chemical plants added more hazards. Some facilities were damaged in the storm. Some caused pollution in the process of shutting down operations to prevent worse damage. At one plant, in order to avoid a fire, workers released a toxic cloud of chemicals. The release forced 200 people to evacuate from their homes.

Nearby, people suffered from the toxic smog. Houston resident Bryan Parras said, "It feels like someone has a hand on the crest of your nose and is pushing down on your nose and eyes. You start to get headaches, your eyes start itching, your throat gets scratchy."[3]

> **"Everywhere you turned, there would just be a new flowing puddle. It just kept filling. . . . I was so scared. We didn't know what would happen. And there is no one you can call."[2]**
>
> *—Maya Wadler, age seventeen, on the flooding of her family's Texas home during Hurricane Harvey*

Worsened by Poverty

A year after Harvey, Herb Mitchell, a staffer in the Texas legislature, commented on the recovery. "Let me say this," he said. "Certain areas of Houston have been taken care of, and certain others have not."[4]

Former Houston mayor Bill White's home, built on stilts above a bayou, flooded during Harvey. As water rose 10 feet (3 m) to the deck of his house, then soaked the first floor, he waded to safety carrying a backpack of belongings. With insurance and savings, White paid to have his ruined first floor gutted and rebuilt. While repairs were made, he stayed in a friend's guesthouse. A year later, his house looked as good as new.

Monika Houston's one-story home was ruined in the storm, too. But without savings or insurance, her family wasn't able to repair it. "We've never been in a position to save," she said. "We've been struggling, trying to hold onto what we have."[5] She received some help from volunteers, the government, and nonprofit groups, but not enough to make the home livable. Twelve months after the storm, she was semi-homeless, shuttling between a trailer on the front lawn and the damaged homes of family and friends.

A survey showed these differences in recovery fall along racial lines. A year after the storm, 27 percent of Hispanic people whose homes were badly damaged said their homes remained unsafe to live in, compared to 20 percent of black people and 11 percent of white people with hurricane-damaged homes. Elena Marks, president and chief executive of the Episcopal Health Foundation, summed up the way Harvey intensified existing hardships: "The farther behind you were before the storm, the less likely you are to bounce back after the storm."[6]

Complex Causes and Effects

Hurricanes are generally seen as natural disasters, caused by Earth's systems rather than by human activity. But the damage in Houston had human causes, too. Houston was once surrounded by abundant open prairie with deep-rooted plants. That landscape could absorb impressive amounts of water. But the city has grown quickly, and people have replaced prairie with pavement, which water can't sink into.

Further, global climate change complicates the job of calling a weather event either "natural" or "human-caused." Global climate change (sometimes called global warming) likely made Harvey's pounding of Houston longer and more severe. Since global climate change is a result of human activity, weather catastrophes such as Harvey have a human-driven cause, too.

People also classify catastrophes according to their effects. An environmental catastrophe is one that primarily damages ecosystems. A humanitarian or human catastrophe primarily harms humans. But these aren't simple black-or-white labels; this hurricane, like many catastrophes, affected the environment as well as human lives.

Common Patterns

For Houston residents, this catastrophe was one of a kind. But Harvey also had much in common with other catastrophes. A catastrophe—a tragic event—may be related to war, disease, weather, cruelty, greed,

Hurricanes are among the most destructive natural catastrophes on the planet. They inflict serious damage on people, property, and the environment.

or chance. It may happen suddenly or slowly. It may affect people's mental or physical health, lives, or property; the survival of an ecosystem or culture; or all of the above.

Whatever its nature, the causes and effects of a disaster are often complex and hard to classify. Often, a catastrophe sets off a cascade of secondary problems. And, as with Harvey, people and communities with fewer resources often bear the brunt of catastrophes and take longer to recover.

Chapter 1

How Have Natural Disasters Affected the Planet?

N atural disasters happen without regard for who's in their way. The weather doesn't obey state or national borders. Shifting tectonic plates don't care about a nation's power or powerlessness. A virus, given the chance, will infect a wealthy person and a poor person equally well.

But the same type of disaster often affects different places differently. A 2016 United Nations (UN) study of more than 7,000 catastrophes found that wealthier countries bear greater financial costs after natural disasters. But it also found that, in poorer countries, the average death toll for each disaster is five times higher than in wealthier countries. As former UN Secretary-General Ban Ki-Moon put it, "High-income countries suffer huge economic losses in disasters, but people in low-income countries pay with their lives."[7]

The devastating twenty-first century earthquakes in Japan (2011) and Haiti (2010) illustrate this difference, with greater financial losses in Japan and much greater loss of life and a more difficult recovery in Haiti. When Hurricane Irma, one of many record-breaking Atlantic storms in the 2010s, struck Caribbean islands as well as the US mainland, people experienced the catastrophe and the recovery

Places like Port-au-Prince, Haiti, are particularly vulnerable to natural disasters. The existing poverty can worsen the effects and aftermath of a catastrophe.

differently, depending on the resources available to them. And the largest-ever outbreak of the deadly Ebola virus, centered in West Africa in 2014, was fought off with long, hard effort and much loss of life in Africa, but much more quickly and with fewer human losses in the developed world.

Earthquake, Haiti, 2010

As 2010 dawned, Haiti was already among the poorest nations in the western hemisphere. More than half the population lived in poverty. The literacy rate was under 50 percent. The health care, housing, transportation, and communication systems were fragile. The country's political history was full of violence and upheaval. Then, on January 12, a 7.0 magnitude earthquake struck. It was Haiti's worst earthquake in more than 200 years.

Frantz Florestal, who lived through the quake in Haiti's capital, Port-au-Prince, described the shaking and the immediate destruction. "You heard the noise under the ground and it's shaking and shaking, and everybody started running. Houses were falling and falling, all of the fences were falling, people were falling, people were crying."[8] Buildings shook to pieces. Landslides wiped out entire communities and destroyed crops and irrigation canals.

> **"We live under a tarp that was ripped by the wind. My children are walking around naked and shoeless. We have no food to eat."[9]**
>
> —*Diera Louis on life in Haiti after the earthquake*

Up to 316,000 people died in the quake, and 1.5 million people were left without shelter. An estimated 300,000 people were injured. And, with damage to agriculture and transportation systems, 3.3 million people faced food shortages. Diera Louis, whose family made a makeshift home in one of 1,300 tent cities, said, "We live under a tarp that was ripped by the wind. My children are walking around naked and shoeless. We have no food to eat."[9]

A cascade of secondary catastrophes followed the earthquake. International aid workers who came to help in the recovery inadvertently brought with them a disease, cholera, that sickened one million Haitians and killed 10,000. Haiti had not had an outbreak of cholera in at least fifty years. But, due to lack of sanitation and clean water, this outbreak lasted for years after the quake.

In the months after the quake, political unrest over a disputed national election added to the country's misery and made recovery even more difficult. Those who tried to help were often unsuccessful, corrupt, or both. The American Red Cross, which raised nearly half a billion dollars from the public to help Haiti, was accused of misusing funds, spending money primarily on administrative expenses, and making little progress. Kim Bolduc, UN Humanitarian Coordinator, said, "This emergency is probably the most complex in history."[10]

A series of other catastrophes pummeled Haiti in the years after the earthquake, further complicating the recovery. Hurricane Sandy struck the island in 2012. A three-year drought followed. In October 2016, Hurricane Matthew killed at least 1,000 people. Seven years after the earthquake, the UN said 2.5 million people in Haiti were still in need of aid. As of 2017, 55,000 people were still living in camps, many in unsanitary conditions, dreaming of building themselves small houses out of cinder blocks to create a somewhat more stable life.

Earthquake, Tsunami, and Nuclear Accident, Japan, 2011

On March 11, 2011, Japan weathered a 9.0 magnitude earthquake. Centered in the ocean off the country's northeastern coast, it was the fifth-largest earthquake anywhere in the world since the year 1900 and the most powerful quake ever recorded in Japan. Toshiaki Takahashi, age forty-nine, lived through the earthquake in the city of Sendai. "I never experienced such a strong earthquake in my life," he

The 2011 earthquake and tsunami caused severe damage to the surrounding area. The enormous waves were powerful enough to carry boats onto city streets.

said. "I thought it would stop, but it just kept shaking and shaking, and getting stronger."[11] Even in Tokyo, more than 200 miles (320 km) from the worst of the damage, the quake was felt intensely. William M. Tsutsui, a professor from the United States who was visiting Tokyo at the time, said, "What was scariest was to look up at the skyscrapers all around," he said. "They were swaying like trees in the breeze."[12]

The earthquake agitated the ocean, causing a tsunami. Waves as high as 130 feet (40 m) swept onto the land, flattening thousands of homes, flooding vast stretches of land, and carrying tons of debris out to sea. Together, the quake and tsunami killed 18,490 people and left

250,000 people without homes. They destroyed 138,000 buildings. The economic cost of this damage was estimated at $360 billion.

As Japan reeled from the quake and the flooding, a third catastrophe unfolded. The earthquake and tsunami cut off power to the reactors at the Fukushima Daiichi nuclear power plant. This disabled the cooling systems. As a result, the reactors overheated, leading to fires, explosions, and the meltdown of fuel in three of the reactors. Nearly half a million people had to evacuate from the area near the plant due to radiation leaks.

Even in the face of such destruction, some parts of disaster recovery happened relatively quickly. Within a couple of weeks of the quake, many damaged highways had been repaired and reopened. Japan Railways had restored rail service between Tokyo and Sendai within a month. Right away, temporary homes for displaced people were under construction.

Japan's central government put about $206 billion into reconstruction and radiation cleanup. Even so, some parts of the recovery have taken years. For example, the town of Otsuchi incorporated quake preparation into its rebuilding process. Otsuchi is being rebuilt on land elevated a full 7 feet (2.1 m) from where it was before and shielded from the ocean by a 48-foot (14.6-m) wall.

In the area affected by radiation from Fukushima Daiichi, as many as 70,000 people were still unable to return to their homes by 2018. Parts of the area were still so contaminated with radiation it may be decades before people can live there again. And contaminated water continued to leak from the nuclear plant into the ocean for many months after the quake. Officials insist that this leakage didn't create direct health hazards for people. But fishing in the area was restricted. And, on land and in the sea, animals and plants have been exposed to high levels of radiation.

Some reconstruction in the tsunami-affected area was still not complete even years after the disaster. Many areas have been overwhelmed by all that needs to be done and are slow to use all the available funds. By 2015, 87,000 people were still living in small, temporary apartments that were originally meant to last only two or three years. Many others had given up waiting and moved away from the quake-affected areas to other parts of Japan. Hiromi Kawaguchi, age sixty-six, lost his wife, mother, and grandson to the tsunami. In 2015, he was still living in a two-room apartment built as refugee housing. He said, "Everyone seems to think that life has gone back to normal here, but we are still very much a disaster zone."[13]

> **"Everyone seems to think that life has gone back to normal here, but we are still very much a disaster zone."[13]**
>
> *—Hiromi Kawaguchi, Japan earthquake survivor, four years after the quake*

Ebola Outbreak, West Africa, 2014–2016

"Ebola is a bad guy," said Foday Gallah. "The pain, it makes you want to give up. I used to be a strong man, and this just broke me down."[14] Gallah, an ambulance supervisor in the African nation of Liberia, was exposed to the Ebola virus while working to save the life of a four-year-old boy. He spent two weeks in an Ebola treatment center, wracked with pain, diarrhea, and fever. He was lucky to survive. More than one-half of people infected in the same outbreak died.

Rebecca Johnson, who survived Ebola in Sierra Leone, described how it felt to be sick with the disease. "I could not walk," she wrote. "I was blind, paralyzed, unable to talk or eat. I had a sore throat, body

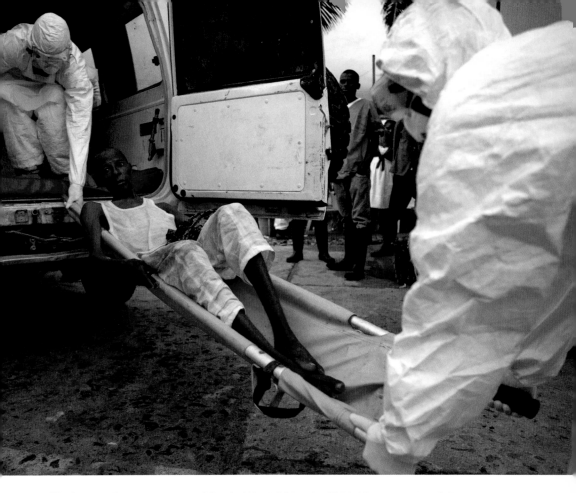

Ebola struck poor communities in West Africa in 2014. The poverty of the affected areas made the disease's effects much more severe.

aches, and my whole body itched. Blood started coming out of my eyes. I couldn't sleep. I was awake with pain all of the time. Once, my soul left my body. I saw my body lying down. I almost went insane. I thought, I am going to die, I will not make it. Every single day I cried."[15]

Ebola is a deadly virus with no reliable cure. Health researchers think the virus lives mainly in wild animal populations—for example, in primates and bats. When a person comes in contact with an infected animal and is infected with the virus, an outbreak begins. Body fluids from people who are sick (or from those who have died of Ebola) are highly contagious and infect people who touch them.

Before 2014, Ebola had only affected small groups of people at once, and outbreaks had happened only in isolated, rural areas, mainly in central Africa. Only 2,361 Ebola cases had ever been reported. But in 2014, Ebola broke out in West Africa for the first time. Most people in the region were not familiar with the virus or how to stop its spread. The disease also reached crowded cities for the first time, giving the virus opportunities to infect more people. At the junction of Sierra Leone, Liberia, and Guinea, people travel frequently across national borders, so the illness spread quickly from Guinea to neighboring countries.

The disease also spread to seven other countries, including the United States. In all, 28,652 cases of Ebola and 11,325 deaths were reported. Because many Ebola cases and deaths probably were not reported to authorities, the actual total number of people affected may be two or three times that. It was, by far, the largest outbreak of Ebola ever.

Most of the impact of the epidemic fell in West Africa. All but fifteen of the deaths were in Guinea, Liberia, and Sierra Leone, and it was two and a half years before all three countries were declared Ebola-free. In the United States and other developed countries where travelers brought the virus, doctors and health authorities were able to keep the virus from affecting many more people and stop the outbreak within weeks.

Why the Difference?

Richer countries had the money and preparation to act quickly and stop the disease from spreading. For example, when the first Ebola patient entered the United States, public health workers were immediately able to track down every person who might have had contact with him, inform them about symptoms to look for, and catch any future cases at the earliest sign of illness. Virtually every community in the United States has running water and a well-stocked hospital or clinic where patients can be kept isolated

Vaccines and Medicines for Ebola

Before the 2014 Ebola outbreak, scientists had spent some time trying to create vaccines and medicines to prevent and treat the disease. But none were yet widely available. So people had to rely only on sanitation and isolation to stop the spread of the disease. And, once a person was sick, there were few treatment options other than fluids and pain relief.

The urban, international outbreak of 2014 brought attention and funding back to the search for solutions. And in 2015, a vaccine trial in Guinea was very successful. None of the at-risk people who received the vaccine became infected. In May 2018, people in the Democratic Republic of the Congo (DRC) began using the same vaccine to control an active Ebola outbreak. The amount of vaccine available was limited, so it was only given to the people with the highest risk: health care workers, people responsible for burying the dead, and people close to those who were sick with the disease.

In November of that year, the DRC started a trial, the first of its kind, to provide and compare four different medicines to treat Ebola. The trial aimed to improve the odds of survival for people affected by this outbreak. It was designed to help scientists know more about which treatments are most effective. By 2019, the outbreak in the DRC had not reached anywhere near the size of the 2014 catastrophe. World Health Organization Director-General Tedros Adhanom Ghebreyesus said, "We hope to one day say that the death and suffering from Ebola is behind us."

Quoted in Colin Dwyer, "Ebola Treatment Trials Launched in Democratic Republic of the Congo Amid Outbreak," NPR, November 27, 2018. www.npr.org.

to avoid sickening others. Transportation, communication, and medical systems are generally strong. And, in general, people trust doctors and public health authorities, allowing all of these parts to work together.

In West Africa, on the other hand, many hospitals and clinics lack running water, soap, and gloves. At the time of the outbreak, Liberia had fewer than 250 doctors for about four million people. Sierra Leone had just 136 doctors for about six million people, and twelve of them died of Ebola. There was a shortage of the protective suits that health workers needed to wear. These conditions made it much more difficult to contain the virus.

Dr. Senga Omeonga, who survived Ebola in Liberia, described the scene in the clinic where he stayed while ill: "For one week I had my bed in the hallway. . . . At that time there was one toilet. But because a lot of people were using it . . . it overflowed and clogged. 'Poo poo' all over the floor. So when I wanted to use the bathroom, there was no way. We just stand at the door."[16]

Hurricane Irma, Caribbean Islands and Florida, 2017

"It's incredible it stayed so fast for so long," said Phil Klotzbach, a hurricane expert at Colorado State University.[17] That sums up the most stunning quality of the 2017 hurricane known as Irma. The storm kept up wind speeds of 185 miles per hour (298 km/h) for thirty-seven hours—the longest period of winds of that speed ever measured. "It was angry," said one survivor. "That's what it sounded like to me. When the roof came off, there were these horrible screeches, this horrible noise. It was devastating, and we all had to run."[18]

Irma struck land in seven places, including many of the northern Caribbean Islands, the Florida Keys, and southwestern Florida.

The storm directly caused ten deaths in the United States and thirty-seven deaths across the Caribbean islands. It caused $51 billion in damage, making it one of the costliest hurricanes on record.

The tiny island of Barbuda suffered the worst damage. High winds and flooding damaged 90 percent of Barbuda's homes and buildings, 40 percent of its roads, and its entire electrical system. All 1,600 people who lived on Barbuda had to evacuate to nearby, larger Antigua, and most were unable to return by 2018. Of the destruction on Barbuda, UN Secretary-General António Guterres said, "I have never seen anywhere else in the world a forest completely decimated without one single leaf on any tree. . . . In every community, most of the buildings are destroyed or heavily damaged."[19] Barbuda resident Primrose Thomas spoke about returning to the island after the evacuation: "The first time I came back, I didn't know where to go. I couldn't recognize anywhere. I had to ask for directions to my own house."[20]

Not the Last of Its Kind

For all its severity, Irma wasn't an outlier. It was part of a trend. Just weeks after Hurricane Irma, another severe hurricane, called Maria, struck many of the same communities. During the next hurricane season, even more record-breaking hurricanes took place.

There is clear evidence that climate change plays a role in creating stronger, longer, rainier storms. Warm ocean waters energize storms, and a warmer, more humid atmosphere primes hurricanes to deliver more rain. And many experts predict more of the same. Jennifer Collins, who researches weather and climate at the University of Southern Florida, said in 2018, "I'm sure we'll have more to come. New records may even occur again this year. There's general agreement in the scientific community that the intensity of the strongest storms are increasing."[21]

Twenty-First Century Natural Catastrophes

These four natural catastrophes are landmark events of the first decades of the twenty-first century. The Ebola outbreak, the Haiti and Japan earthquakes, and Hurricane Irma aren't just the largest catastrophes of their kind this century; each of them broke records, either locally or worldwide.

These landmark catastrophes took place in a world where the gap between rich and poor is enormous. And these catastrophes all happened at a time when many events that were once considered natural now include a human-driven component: climate change. These same circumstances—wealth, poverty, and climate change—will keep shaping catastrophes, large and small, that strike in the coming years. Wealth and poverty can make the difference between a bearable recovery period and an ongoing cascade of trauma. Wealth can even make the difference, as in the case of the Ebola outbreak, between a widespread catastrophe and a near miss.

Costliest Hurricanes and Storms of the 2000s

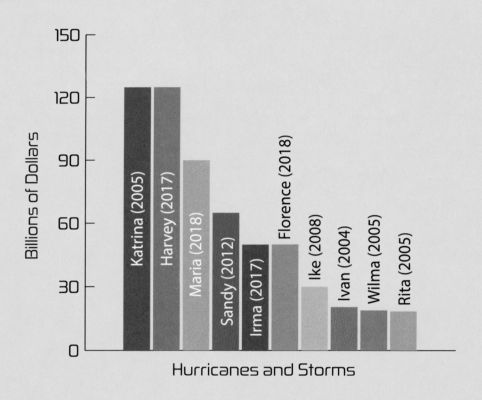

In addition to the human toll, the wind, rainfall, and flooding caused by major storms and hurricanes can cause devastating economic damage to property. Homes, businesses, and infrastructure may have to be repaired or replaced after a storm strikes a community. Experts assess a total dollar value for the damage a storm does. Above are the costliest storms of the 2000s.

"Costliest US Tropical Cyclone Tables," NOAA, 2018. www.nhc.noaa.gov.

Chapter 2

How Have Catastrophes in Nature Affected the Planet?

Human actions can alter the world around us. And when people are working together to handle large amounts of hazardous substances, from time to time they make mistakes that change things for the worse. This is true whether people are wielding fire to clear land for agriculture, extracting flammable resources from the earth, or disposing of waste. When these things get out of hand, there are consequences. And, ultimately, because human beings are closely connected to their environment, the negative consequences come back to harm people, too. Fortunately, sometimes environmental catastrophes give society a chance to reconsider how we do things and make changes to keep from repeating them.

Deepwater Horizon Oil Spill, Gulf of Mexico, 2010

On April 20, 2010, the Deepwater Horizon ran into trouble. The Horizon, an oil rig, was afloat in the Gulf of Mexico 52 miles (84 km) off the coast of Louisiana, in water 5,000 feet (1,500 m) deep. The Horizon's deck was the size of a football field, and its two lower floors were a floating home for its crew, equipped with sleeping quarters,

The explosion on the Deepwater Horizon created pollution both above and below the water's surface. As smoke poured from the rig, oil gushed into the sea deep underwater.

private bathrooms, and even a gym and a movie theater. On that day, after seventy-four days of drilling, the 126 people on board were close to completing a challenging project: an oil well reaching 13,000 feet (4,000 m) below the ocean floor.

An oil well is a hole drilled far below Earth's surface to reach rock formations that contain oil and natural gas. Since the oil and gas are underneath many tons of rock with nowhere to flow out, they're under pressure. Drill rigs are designed to push back against the pressure of the liquid and gas inside the rock formation, releasing it in a controlled way as the liquid and gas are extracted. When the pressure inside the well isn't controlled properly, the result is what drillers call a blowout. The liquid and gas in the rock formation flow up and out with great force.

That's what happened on the Deepwater Horizon. First, inside the rig, water and mud erupted up and out of the well, spraying with incredible force. The blowout was so loud it sounded like a jet engine. As the crew scrambled to stop the blowout, not just water and mud but also flammable methane gas ripped their way out of the well. The methane filled the rig and, within minutes, ignited in two enormous explosions.

The explosions created a fireball hundreds of feet high. Greg Meche, a crew member who had served in the military in Iraq, said, "I never heard a bomb like that in Baghdad."[22] For crew members who were working far from the well itself, the explosions came without warning. Kenneth Roberts was washing dishes when the blasts happened. They knocked him out. "I woke up under a table," he said.[23]

> **"I never heard a bomb like that in Baghdad."[22]**
>
> —Greg Meche, Iraq War veteran and Deepwater Horizon crew member, on the explosion aboard the oil rig

Flames and more explosions engulfed the giant rig. The crew tried many emergency measures to bring the blowout and fire under control, but within minutes it became clear they would need to abandon the rig to survive. Matt Jacobs, a firefighter on board, said the scene was "like staring into the face of death."[24]

Many crew members escaped in lifeboats; some jumped overboard to escape the burning ship. Altogether, 115 people survived. They left behind eleven dead crewmates whose bodies would never be recovered, a fire burning out of control, and a well still uncontrollably spewing oil and gas into the waters of the Gulf of Mexico.

It took eighty-seven days to stop the flow of oil into the ocean. An estimated total of 4.9 million barrels (154.3 million gallons or 584.2 million L) of oil spilled into the sea. It was the largest oil spill in US history. The oil killed uncountable sea creatures and other wildlife and dirtied more than 1,300 miles (2,100 km) of coastline. It's estimated that nearly one million seabirds died. The tourism and fishing industries suffered major financial losses.

There's evidence that the spill also had long-term effects on microscopic ocean life. In 2018 a team of University of Southern Mississippi scientists studied the diversity of microbes in the gulf. They discovered that near the spill site, fewer types of microbes were present compared to before the spill. Leila Hamdan, the lead researcher, said, "It's premature to imagine that all the effects of the spill are over and remediated."[25] She explained that deep sea microbes recycle nutrients. There could be large, longer-term consequences to such a large disruption of their health.

Why Did It Happen?

For years after the Deepwater Horizon catastrophe, people worked to figure out why the blowout, fire, and spill happened. Robert Bea, an engineering professor at the University of California, Berkeley,

The oil spill caused considerable damage to nearby coastal communities. In its aftermath, people living in the area protested against British Petroleum, the company that operated the oil rig.

summed up the complexity of the disaster: "It was a chain of important errors made by people in critical situations involving complex technological and organization systems."[26]

Many factors contributed to the catastrophe. A key piece of equipment called a blowout preventer failed in several ways. The blowout preventer was overdue for a safety inspection. The company did not have well-thought-out plans in place for such a disaster. A key emergency disconnect system on the rig failed to work. The crew was under pressure to work quickly and complete the job. They chose not to take certain safety measures because they didn't want to cause costly delays by overreacting to what could be just a small problem. In the end, British Petroleum (BP) was found to bear most of the blame for the disaster. The company was subjected to tens of billions of dollars in fines to pay for the cleanup and compensate people affected by the spill.

In 2016, in response to this catastrophe, the US federal government tightened the rules about blowout preventers and other safety devices. A government statement at the time said the rules aimed to "protect workers' lives and the environment from the potentially devastating effects of blowouts and offshore oil spills."[27] In 2018, a new presidential administration repealed those regulations. It issued a new, looser policy instead. The administration said that the previous regulations created burdens for the oil and gas industry without increasing workers' safety or protecting the environment.

Mega Forest Fires, Indonesia, 2015

Indonesia's forests are some of the most biodiverse places on Earth. And Indonesia produces more palm oil, pulpwood (wood for making paper), and timber than any other country in the world. In 2015, these forests experienced an environmental catastrophe. Between June and October, wildfires burned throughout the country, devastating 6.4 million acres (25,900 million sq km) of forest and farmland.

The fastest, cheapest way to prepare land for farming is a technique called slash-and-burn, which involves using fire to clear the land. In 2011, the Indonesian government outlawed this type of land clearing in many areas. There had already long been concerns in the country about loss of forests when the fires got out of hand. But, even after slash-and-burn rules were in place, fires kept happening in the restricted areas and many others. In 2015, due to especially dry weather, the fires were even harder to control than usual. Much of the soil in Indonesia is peat, a rich and flammable type of organic matter. That year, the soil was dry not only from lack of rain but also, in some places, from years of having moisture sucked out by drainage canals. In the relatively dry peat, fires smoldered for days, spread easily, and were impossible to stop until the rainy season arrived.

The fires spewed a smoky haze across much of the country and neighboring Malaysia and Singapore, as well as hundreds of miles away in southern Thailand. Poor visibility and poor air quality kept planes from flying and caused schools to be closed for weeks. Scientists say it was the worst period of fires and haze ever recorded. At the peak of the fires, NASA satellites photographed more than 130,000 fire hotspots spanning the country. Because the fires spread deep into dense, wild areas and national parks, countless living creatures and their habitats were destroyed.

When Indonesia's forests are harmed, the indigenous people who rely on the forests are threatened as well. Bepak Pengusai, a leader of the Orang Rimba, one of Indonesia's indigenous groups, said that the well-being of his people is closely tied to the forest. "If there's no forest," he said, "there's no Orang Rimba and the other way round."[28]

The haze also caused discomfort and health issues for people far from the forests. One resident of Palangkaraya, Indonesia, reported, "We have days we call 'Hari Kuning' ('yellow days'). This is when the dense, sound-deadening smog somehow absorbs the light from the invisible sun, turning everything a surreal sepia color."[29]

The small particles in smoke and haze can cause asthma, bronchitis, lung cancer, and heart disease. Reports shortly after the fire stated that the poor air quality caused nineteen deaths and around a half million respiratory infections in Indonesia, as well as illnesses in Singapore and Malaysia. In 2016, researchers from Harvard University and Columbia University published a study showing that the effects were probably much worse. The researchers estimated that 91,600 people in Indonesia, 6,500 in Malaysia, and 2,200 in Singapore may have died prematurely because of the pollution.

> **"We have days we call 'Hari Kuning' ('yellow days'). This is when the dense, sound-deadening smog somehow absorbs the light from the invisible sun, turning everything a surreal sepia color."[29]**
>
> —*Resident of Palangkaraya, Indonesia, on living with the haze from the 2015 wildfires*

Since 2015, Indonesia has made tougher laws about slash-and-burn techniques. These new policies include harsher penalties for those who break the laws and a firmer commitment to enforcement. The government has also put money into training local communities to prevent and fight fires. There is some evidence that these regulations have kept fires and haze under better control. Since that catastrophic year, each Indonesian dry season has brought some forest fires. But they've been nowhere near as severe or widespread as the 2015 fires. Still, some have expressed concern that the new rules aren't enforced well enough. Fires have continued to spring up in the very areas the new rules are supposed to protect. And Indonesia hasn't yet experienced another year as dry as 2015, so the real effectiveness of the new laws has yet to be tested.

Great Pacific Garbage Patch, Ongoing

In 1997, Charles Moore was sailing his yacht back to California after competing in a sailboat race in Hawaii. About halfway there, he made a disturbing discovery. He wrote about it later: "[A]s I gazed from the deck at the surface of what ought to have been a pristine ocean, I was confronted, as far as the eye could see, with the sight of plastic. . . . In the week it took to cross . . . no matter what time of day I looked, plastic debris was floating everywhere: bottles, bottle caps, wrappers, fragments."[30]

The area Moore stumbled on came to be called the Great Pacific Garbage Patch. Today, more than twenty years after Moore came upon it, it still exists and is growing quickly. In March 2018, scientists studied the patch. They estimated it consists of at least 87,000 tons (79,000 metric tons) of trash floating in an area twice the size of Texas. The patch contains four to sixteen times more trash than previous studies estimated. Though there's some glass, rubber, and wood, 99.9 percent of the trash is plastic.

At one time, people thought the garbage patch was mainly made of tiny fragments of plastic. But the 2018 study made clear that the bulk of the plastic is in larger pieces, mainly in the form of fishing nets and other abandoned or lost fishing gear. Among the 1.8 trillion pieces of trash are items with origins in North and South America and Asia. As much as 20 percent of the trash may be debris from the 2011 tsunami in Japan. Laurent Lebreton, the main author of the 2018 study, said, "It's just quite alarming, because you are so far from

Plastic trash has become a serious problem in many bodies of water, including the oceans. Currents can carry this waste into concentrated areas.

the mainland. There's no one around and you still see those common objects, like crates and bottles."[31]

Ocean currents move in predictable ways. They're caused by wind patterns and by the force of Earth's rotation. A circular system of ocean currents is called a gyre, and the Great Pacific Garbage Patch is at the center of the North Pacific Subtropical Gyre. This gyre moves clockwise around a 7.7-million-square-mile (20-million-sq-km) area of ocean. As the gyre moves, it draws trash toward its center. At the center the water is calm, and trash accumulates there.

Trash in the ocean can harm the ecosystem in a number of ways. Animals such as sea turtles and albatrosses may mistake plastic and other trash for food, consume it, and die of starvation or ruptured organs. Seals and other mammals may become entangled in abandoned fishing nets or other debris and drown. One study estimated that 100,000 marine animals are injured or killed by plastics every year.

Plastic debris in the ocean may also disrupt the oceanic food chain from the bottom up. Fragments of floating plastic can keep light from reaching algae and plankton, the tiny organisms that are the main food source for much ocean life. If algae and plankton can't thrive, the food supply suffers all the way up the food chain, meaning scarce resources for fish and marine mammals as well as for humans who eat seafood.

The substances plastics may carry are another concern. As sunlight and wave action break plastic trash into smaller and smaller pieces, the plastic releases some of the chemicals it's made of, including dyes and bisphenol A (BPA), which has been linked to health problems. Plastic trash can also soak up other pollutants that may be present in the ocean. So when animals eat plastic trash, they may be taking in concentrated amounts of those pollutants. This affects the entire food chain as well.

The garbage patch is hundreds of miles from any land, and no country or government has taken responsibility for cleaning it up. But the Ocean Cleanup Foundation, a nonprofit founded by a Dutch inventor, has made this cleanup its mission. Joost Dubois, a representative of the foundation, says, "It's a ticking time bomb of

Teenager's Inspiration Becomes Ocean Solution

On a snorkeling trip to Greece, teenaged tinkerer Boyan Slat ran into an unpleasant surprise. Floating through the gorgeous blue water, he ran into more garbage than fish. Trash in the ocean immediately struck him as a problem he wanted to solve. "I always had my projects," he said, "but they weren't very useful. And that really changed when I found this problem." Back at home in the Netherlands, he got to work designing a contraption to clean garbage out of the ocean. The first version he designed was for a high school science project.

After studying engineering in college, he decided to dedicate himself full-time to solving the problem of ocean trash. He had only about 300 Euros (about US $340) to work with. He emailed several hundred companies to ask them to sponsor his work. Only one company replied— to say it was a terrible idea. But Boyan didn't quit. He successfully crowdfunded his work to found the Ocean Cleanup Foundation and, with a team, built a machine that cleans up ocean trash. The team ran into plenty of difficulties along the way. Frustratingly, they had to scrap their first design because they couldn't make it work. But at last they completed an elegant system that does the job.

Their system launched in September 2018. Eventually, Boyan hopes the project will fund itself. Plastic trash from the ocean will be brought back to shore and recycled into desirable products whose sales will fund further cleanup efforts.

Quoted in "How Boyan Slat's Ocean Cleanup Was Derailed by a Flawed Design," YouTube, September 7, 2018. www.youtube.com.

larger material. We've got to get it before it breaks down into a size that's too small to collect and also dangerous for marine life."[32]

In September 2018 the Ocean Cleanup Foundation launched a system that, if it works, will remove about 150,000 pounds (68,000 kg) of plastic per year, doing away with about half of the garbage patch in five years. The system is a U-shaped set of floating booms. It moves along on the current and traps garbage so that a ship can pick it up and return it to land to be sorted and recycled. The cleanup will likely cost about $32 million.

There are some concerns about the cleanup. Some people are worried that the floating contraption itself may attract and endanger marine life. Another concern is that cleaning up the garbage patch may not address the real problem. The garbage patch has attracted a lot of attention in the news because its size and scale are impressive. The larger problem, though, says Eben Schwartz, marine debris program manager for the California Coastal Commission, is that people keep adding more plastic to the ocean every day. "What's floating on the surface of the ocean gyres is only three percent of the plastics that enters the ocean every single year," he said. "The solution to plastic pollution entering our ocean starts on land."[33]

> **"What's floating on the surface of the ocean gyres is only three percent of the plastics that enters the ocean every single year. . . . The solution to plastic pollution entering our ocean starts on land."[33]**
>
> —*Eben Schwartz, marine debris program manager for the California Coastal Commission*

Twenty-First Century Environmental Catastrophes

The world's population is growing quickly, and the world's total energy use climbs every year. So it makes sense that some of humans' biggest impacts on the environment come from our need for energy. The Deepwater Horizon oil spill was a direct result of energy use. In the nuclear reactor meltdown caused by the 2011 Japan earthquake and tsunami, the need for energy was also a driver of the catastrophe.

Like natural catastrophes, environmental catastrophes this century are often entangled with climate change. If the Deepwater Horizon's drilling mission had been successful, the result would have been oil and gas to burn. This activity adds carbon to the atmosphere and contributes to climate change. Burning peat releases carbon as well. Indonesia's 2015 fire season released more carbon into the atmosphere than Japan releases in an entire year. So, in that case, one environmental disaster contributed to another. The reverse might also be true; climate change may have contributed to the dry weather that led to the extreme wildfires.

The Pacific garbage patch doesn't directly connect to climate change, but it does carry a lesson that might apply to many kinds of environmental catastrophes. The garbage gyre would stop growing if people handled their trash more carefully and cut down on how much they use. Considering how human activity will affect the environment is one key to avoiding environmental catastrophes, or at least reducing their impact.

Chapter 3

How Have Human Catastrophes Affected the Planet?

With or without meaning to, through carelessness, hatred, ignorance, or neglect, sometimes people inflict catastrophes on one another. Violence is the most obvious way this happens. But physical harm isn't the only way people create catastrophes. People separate others from their homes or families. They make choices about resources, sometimes in ways that harm others' health and well-being. Even failure to properly care for precious objects can be a catastrophe for a group of people.

Water Crisis, Flint, Michigan, 2014–2018

Only 71 percent of the world's population has a reliable source of safe, clean drinking water. But in wealthy countries such as the United States, most people trust that tap water is free of bacteria and toxins and is safe to drink. However, the city of Flint, Michigan, can no longer take clean water as a given.

Flint's water catastrophe began in April 2014. For more than fifty years, the city had used water from Lake Huron, treated by the Detroit water system. That spring, Flint's leaders decided to use a different,

As the scope of Flint's water problem became clear, it attracted national attention. Members of Congress spoke out about it and proposed legislation to address the crisis.

less expensive water source, the Flint River, and purify the water using the city's own treatment plant. Almost immediately after the switch, people in Flint noticed that something was wrong. The water smelled bad. It tasted like metal. It came out of the faucet looking orange or red, murky, and foamy. Sometimes there were particles floating in it. People reported skin rashes and hair loss.

For many months, citizens of Flint told city and state officials about these concerns. They attended public meetings. They sent petitions and letters. Flint resident Jan Burgess wrote, "The water is not safe to drink, cook, or wash dishes with, or even give to pets. We worry every time we shower."[34] Over and over for many months, officials gave the people of Flint the same answer. They told them there was nothing to worry about. They said the water was perfectly safe to drink.

The foul-smelling, dirty-looking water persisted. And more problems cropped up. Several cases of Legionnaires' disease, a type of pneumonia carried in contaminated water, emerged in Flint. In response, authorities issued some temporary warnings about the water, always claiming, after a short time, that the water was safe again. In January 2015, the city also issued a notice saying that the water had a high level of trihalomethanes (THMs), chemicals that can increase the risk of cancer and other diseases. The notice said that there was no emergency. It assured people the problem would be fixed.

The people of Flint remained concerned. One resident said, "I don't know how it can be clean if it smells and tastes bad."[35] In March 2015, the lead level in one resident's water was found to be 397 parts per billion. Lead is a health hazard. Especially in children, it can cause irreversible health, developmental, and behavioral problems. Scientists say that any amount of lead can be harmful, but US clean water laws require action if the level is higher than fifteen parts per billion. The level in Flint was twenty-six times that amount.

The source of all of the trouble, it became clear, was corrosion. Most water treatment plants add an anti-corrosion agent to the water supply. This gives water pipes a protective coating and keeps them

Laboratory testing helped demonstrate how serious the Flint water crisis was. A research team from Virginia Tech was central to this work.

from disintegrating. The Flint water treatment plant didn't add this agent, so the water corroded the pipes as it flowed. This changed the makeup of the water, causing the bad taste, smell, and appearance, the growth of the bacteria that causes Legionnaires' disease, and the high lead levels.

Only in October 2015 did Flint take action and switch back to the Detroit water source. But the city's water pipes remained corroded and kept releasing contaminants into the water system. In January 2016, the federal and state governments approved aid for Flint. The state provided free bottled water for residents for two years. Other emergency funding helped Flint replace all of the city's corroded water lines, a project that, by October 2018, was only about 75 percent complete.

The long-term health results of the contaminated water in Flint are still unfolding. The water sickened at least ninety people with Legionnaires' disease, and twelve people died of the illness. Flint residents, including children, were exposed to unhealthy levels of lead. The effects of lead ingestion are irreversible. During the water crisis, the fetal death rate in Flint also increased by 58 percent.

An independent task force worked to sort out who was to blame for the disaster. In March 2016, it issued its final report, saying the main responsibility lay with the Michigan Department of Environmental Quality (MDEQ). The report says that, when presented with complaints about Flint's water, MDEQ's "response was often one of aggressive dismissal, belittlement, and attempts to discredit these efforts and the individuals involved."[36]

Several MDEQ employees resigned. Four officials faced criminal charges related to the crisis. Prosecutors argued that the officials were in a position to notify the public about the hazardous water and fix the problem sooner than they did. And, in July 2018, the Environmental Protection Agency's (EPA's) Office of the Inspector General called on the EPA to take a more active role in enforcing water quality standards.

Flint is an economically poor city. Its economy relied on the auto industry, and as that industry has declined, many businesses and many people have left town. Of Flint's nearly 100,000 people, more than 40 percent live in poverty. More than one-half of the population is black. Many people believe that such a crisis would not have been allowed to happen (or to go on as long) in a city with more money or in a mostly white community. Flint resident Kaleka Lewis Harris said, "I probably—honestly, I feel like it was done on purpose because Flint is predominantly black. . . . A government that's predominantly white . . . showed me what they feel about me and us here in Flint. They showed us."[37]

> **"I do not believe it. The trust is gone. The trust is gone for everybody."[38]**
>
> —Flint resident Kaleka Lewis Harris on being told Flint's water is now safe to drink

In October 2018, officials were once again declaring Flint's water safe to drink. But many people in Flint still have a hard time trusting that claim. Harris said, "I do not believe it. The trust is gone. The trust is gone for everybody."[38] As of October 2018, many people in Flint were still drinking bottled water— often donated by companies and charities.

Rohingya Persecution, Myanmar, 2017

In August and September 2017, more than 700,000 Rohingya people fled the country of Myanmar. They carried nearly nothing. They were traumatized and terrified. They left the country by land and by sea. Some, packed onto rickety rafts, drowned on the way. They fled into neighboring Bangladesh, where they gathered in vast camps. After learning about what caused them to flee, UN mission chair Marzuki Darusman said, "I have never been confronted by crimes as horrendous and on such a scale as these."[39]

During those terrible days, soldiers entered Rohingya villages in Myanmar. They tortured, disfigured, raped, abused, and killed Rohingya people and destroyed their villages. They used knives, grenades, guns, and fire. Not only soldiers but also neighboring Buddhist villagers participated in the horrors. Mohammad Rayes, a twenty-three-year-old teacher, escaped his village alive by climbing and hiding in a tree. But he saw what happened. "People were screaming, crying, pleading for their lives," he said, "but the soldiers just shot continuously."[40]

> **"People were screaming, crying, pleading for their lives, but the soldiers just shot continuously."[40]**
>
> —*Mohammad Rayes, survivor of Rohingya persecution in Myanmar*

Satellite images show that 400 villages were burned. An estimated 25,000 people were killed. The exact number of people lost may never be known, because Myanmar will not let outside observers into the affected areas. The Myanmar government denies that these crimes happened. They insist that the military did not harm civilians. They say they were only punishing a militant group called the Arakan Rohingya Salvation Army (ARSA), which attacked several police outposts in August 2017. They claim the Rohingya burned their own villages and faked the massacres.

At the beginning of 2017, about one million Rohingya people lived in Myanmar. The Rohingya consider Myanmar their homeland. They've lived there for many generations. But they're Muslims, and Myanmar is a majority-Buddhist country with a Buddhist government. Because of this, Myanmar's government has refused, for the past thirty years, to recognize the Rohingya as citizens. Instead, the government says they are illegal immigrants from Bangladesh. Myanmar's fear and hatred of

Art and Recovering from Catastrophes

In 2018, Max Frieder and Joel Bergner, two New York artists, visited the Kutupalong refugee camp in Bangladesh. Their goal was to share art with Rohingya refugees. The two artists run an organization called Artolution. They've traveled widely, painting murals with people in conflict zones.

They spent several weeks at Kutupalong. With the help of hundreds of interested children, teenagers, and families, they created more than a dozen murals. The colorful art is a welcome addition to a camp crowded with bamboo-and-tarp shelters. Since there aren't enough schools or jobs for everyone in the camp, people also welcomed the chance to work together and make something beautiful.

In May, the Rohingya artists sent a gift back to New York: a mural painted by children and adults living in the camp. The mural was brought to New York City and displayed in the World Trade Center transit hub, where about a half million people could see it every day. Frieder said, "I think people around the world have no idea who the Rohingya people are and what they are going through. These pieces of art, these stories that they create, are able to say, 'we are here, we exist.'"

Quoted in Rishabh R. Jain, "2 New Yorker Artists Bring Colors, Smiles to Rohingya Camps," AP News, November 27, 2018. www.apnews.com.

the Rohingya has deep historical roots and had risen for years before the 2017 horrors. The origins of this conflict reach back to World War II (1939–1945) and the Rohingya's fight, after the war, for their own homeland.

In the years leading up to the August 2017 crisis, the military and other Buddhists in Myanmar used many avenues, including Facebook, to spread hatred and lies about the Rohingya. The military posted photos of dismembered children, falsely claiming that Muslim terrorists

Injured Rohingya refugees walk through a refugee camp in Bangladesh. They were among hundreds of thousands of people displaced by the crisis.

killed them. Maung Thway Chun, the editor of a Buddhist newspaper, said, "We don't want Muslims to swallow our country. . . . It is such a shame for us that the land we inherited from our former generations will be lost in our time."[41] In reality, only 4 percent of Myanmar is Muslim. The persecution targeted teachers, religious leaders, and other influential people. It seems that Myanmar's goal was to erase Rohingya culture and history entirely. U Kyaw San Hla, a state security ministry officer, said, "There is no such thing as Rohingya. It is fake news."[42]

Even before the crisis, more than 300,000 Rohingya had already left Myanmar to escape persecution and violence. But the flight of the Rohingya out of Myanmar in 2017 was one of the fastest movements of an entire people out of a country in modern history. International aid groups moved quickly to provide the refugees with clean water, sanitation, food, vaccinations, and medical care.

During 2018, the number of Rohingya refugees in Bangladesh grew to one million. Bangladesh, unwilling to host the Rohingya indefinitely, worked with Myanmar to make a plan for the Rohingya to return home. Myanmar agreed to accept 150 Rohingya per day back into the country. In November 2018 the two countries officially opened the possibility of return.

But not a single Rohingya refugee agreed to reenter Myanmar. All indications are that the situation is still just as unsafe for the Rohingya as it was in 2017. Myanmar still refuses to acknowledge that the Rohingya exist as a people. Muslims continue to leave Myanmar for the safety of Bangladesh. And a UN fact-finding mission reported in October 2018, "It is an ongoing genocide."[43]

National Museum Fire, Brazil, 2018

The night of September 2, 2018, a fire broke out at Brazil's Museu Nacional, or National Museum. The fire, most likely caused by problems with the building's electrical wiring, didn't lead to any injuries or deaths. But the entire building was destroyed, and with it 90 percent of the museum's collection of 20 million artifacts. Brazil's president at the time, Michel Temer, called the scale of the loss "incalculable to Brazil." He said, "Two hundred years of work, research and knowledge have been lost."[44] Luiz Rocha, a Brazilian ichthyologist, said of the museum's collections, "They were unique as it gets: Many of them were irreplaceable, there's no way to put a monetary value on it."[45]

The museum housed dinosaur fossils, including many unique to Brazil. It had hundreds of South American artifacts from precolonial times, including a Chilean mummy that was at least 3,500 years old. Many of its natural history specimens, including mollusks and insects, were holotypes, the best or most important examples of a species and a kind of global reference for understanding the species. Also lost was the oldest collection of Egyptian mummies in South America, along with hundreds of other Egyptian artifacts.

Another great loss was the museum's collection of items related to indigenous Brazilian cultures. Some of the museum's art and ceramics came from cultures of which only a few thousand members are still living. There were also audio recordings of people speaking indigenous languages, some of which have no living speakers left. Brazilian anthropologist Mariana Françozo said, "I have no words to say how horrible this is. . . . We can no longer study them, we can no longer understand what our ancestors did. It's heartbreaking."[46]

Ecologist Emilio Bruna often used the museum's collections in his scientific work. But his understanding of this catastrophic loss goes beyond a specific research project. He said, "Those insects pinned in a drawer, or those fish in a jar, or a feathered cape you might see in a display case—that represents a little piece of who we are as a people, as humans, as

> **"I have no words to say how horrible this is. . . . We can no longer study them, we can no longer understand what our ancestors did. It's heartbreaking."[46]**
>
> —Mariana Françozo, anthropologist, on the loss of indigenous language recordings

part of a greater world. And when those specimens are lost, we lose some of who we are."[47]

People often think of fires as natural disasters, but this destructive fire had human causes. The upkeep of the building had been neglected for many years. It had no working sprinkler system to slow or stop the fire. When firefighters arrived, the hydrants outside the building were dry. They had to bring in tankers and fight the fire with water from a nearby lake.

Due in part to economic troubles in Brazil, the museum simply didn't have the money for the maintenance that might have prevented or slowed the fire. Between 2013 and 2017, the museum's funding was cut by about one-third. In 2018, its financial support dropped further still. In 2015, the museum had to close its doors temporarily because it didn't have the money to pay security and cleaning staff. When termites damaged a hall containing dinosaur and whale skeletons, the museum had to resort to crowdfunding to restore it.

A few artifacts survived the blaze. The most notable among these was Luzia, an 11,500-year-old human skull, one of the oldest human fossils ever found in South America. And the many anthropologists, archeologists, botanists, geoscientists, linguists, and zoologists who worked at the museum will continue to do their research and build knowledge. Right after the fire, the office of president Michel Temer said the president had met with representatives from major Brazilian companies and banks to look into ways to help rebuild the museum quickly.

In October, the UN launched an emergency effort to help restore some of the collections. Other museums in at least ten countries plan to support the rebuilding effort by donating items similar to those lost. Indigenous tribes in Brazil may also donate items. Copies of some, but probably not all, of the recordings of indigenous languages may

An aerial view demonstrates the damage done to Brazil's National Museum. A vast collection of priceless artifacts was lost in the fire.

be found in other collections. By late October 2018, the effort to find fragments of lost items in the rubble of the burned building was still ongoing.

An element of uncertainty entered the rebuilding effort with Brazil's October 2018 presidential election. Newly elected president Jair Bolsonaro did not say whether he would support the effort. As a candidate, he pushed to save money by eliminating the Ministry of Culture, a move that would affect the museum's funding. A few days after the fire, the month before he was elected, Bolsonaro answered a reporter's question about the museum: "It caught fire already. What do you want me to do?"[48]

Twenty-First Century Human Catastrophes

These human catastrophes show some of the worst things human beings can do to each other. People can be incredibly violent and brutal. They can forget one another's humanity. They can neglect their responsibility to protect other people's health, safety, security, and sense of well-being. They can be mindless and forget what they all share.

But these twenty-first century human catastrophes also show some of the best human qualities: resilience and compassion. After all the Rohingya people have been through, they are keeping their community alive, and people from many countries have worked together to make sure they have food, medicine, and a safe place to live. The people of Flint kept speaking up until their water supply was on its way back to health. People who loved Brazil's National Museum grieved what they'd lost, then got to work reassembling the body of knowledge. People around the world responded, sharing what they could.

Chapter 4

How Has Climate Change Affected the Planet?

G lobal climate change is wrapped up with many types of catastrophes. The 2015 severe wildfires in Indonesia and the intensity of hurricanes Harvey and Irma were likely influenced by global climate change. And scientists expect that the number and severity of climate-change-related catastrophes will increase in the coming years. This will affect both humans and the rest of the environment.

What Is Global Climate Change?

The average temperature on Earth is increasing rapidly. It's risen by about 1.8°F (1°C) since the late 1800s. Human beings have never before experienced climate change this rapid. Scientists know this is happening—and know how unusual it is—because, using evidence found in ice cores and sediment cores, they have assembled a record of Earth's climate reaching back many thousands of years. Through many decades of studying this data, scientists have learned about Earth's typical pattern of ice ages and warmer periods. They've learned that Earth is warming about ten times faster now than in an average warming period in the past. Scientists are confident that this

Scientists study ice cores to help piece together Earth's climate history. Air bubbles trapped in the long tubes of ice indicate how the atmosphere has changed over time.

warming is not primarily caused by natural climate variations and is instead driven by human activity.

An average temperature difference of a degree or two may sound small. But small changes in temperature are connected to drastic changes in the environment. For example, at the end of the last ice age, the average temperature on Earth was only 5 to 9°F (2.8 to 5°C) cooler than it is now. But, at that time, 3,000 feet (914 m) of ice covered all of what we now call the northeastern United States and much of the Midwest. A few degrees make a big difference, and in some places the temperature increase has already been much greater.

A common point of confusion about climate change has to do with the difference between weather and climate. A person might think that an especially cold winter month or an especially cool summer week means Earth isn't warming after all. It's important to remember that climate has to do with long-term trends in a region or across the whole planet. The weather changes we notice from day to day or week to week happen during a much shorter period of time than climate change does. Climate change is happening over decades. And it's a change in the average temperature across the whole planet. That still leaves plenty of room for occasional cold snaps and even cooler-than-average summers.

Warmer temperatures, along with some of their effects, have been observed and measured all over the world. The oceans have warmed. The polar ice caps are becoming smaller and thinner. The rate of ice loss in Antarctica tripled between 2012 and 2018. Nearly all glaciers in the world are shrinking. Melting ice is causing sea levels to rise nearly twice as quickly as they did in the past century, and they're rising faster every year, leading to coastal flooding and loss of property. These changes are already affecting life on the planet, and scientists predict that more extreme changes—some with catastrophic consequences for humans—will unfold in the coming decades.

What Causes Climate Change?

It's all but certain that humans are causing climate change by burning fossil fuels. When fossil fuels such as coal and oil burn, they release carbon dioxide into the atmosphere. Over the past century, humanity

The release of greenhouse gases is causing climate change. Industrial facilities, such as power plants, are among the biggest sources of these emissions.

has burned fossil fuels to power vehicles and to create electricity for household use, manufacturing, and many other purposes. In the process, people have drastically increased the amount of carbon dioxide in Earth's atmosphere.

When there's more carbon dioxide in Earth's atmosphere, the atmosphere holds in more of the sun's heat and the average temperature on Earth rises. Carbon dioxide is sometimes called a greenhouse gas. Like the insulated glass roof of a greenhouse, an atmosphere rich in carbon dioxide lets the sun's heat in and stops it from reflecting back out.

Thousands of scientists all over the world have spent many decades collecting, studying, and understanding data about Earth's climate. They've gathered an enormous body of information, from ancient climate records found in deep ice cores to images collected by Earth-orbiting satellites. Based on all of these observations taken as a whole, the global scientific community's assessment is this: by burning fossil fuels, humans have added greenhouse gases to the atmosphere, creating an unprecedented change in climate that is having extreme effects on Earth's climate systems.

> **"Observations throughout the world make it clear that climate change is occurring, and rigorous scientific research demonstrates that the greenhouse gases emitted by human activities are the primary driver."[49]**
>
> *—2009 joint statement by eighteen scientific associations*

In 2009, the members of eighteen different US scientific associations signed on to a statement that human activities are the main cause of global climate change: "Observations throughout the world make it clear that climate change is occurring, and rigorous scientific research demonstrates that the greenhouse gases emitted by human activities are the primary driver."[49]

Climate Change and Environmental Catastrophes

Human-driven climate change is happening quickly. And it's quickly changing the rules for living things. Each species of animal, plant, fungus, and even microbe has unique features and behaviors. Each one has adapted to its place within a system of other living things in a relatively stable climate. In an unstable climate, the qualities that once helped an organism survive may no longer work. Species that can't adapt to the new conditions may go extinct—either in one place or globally. Those that do survive will live within a landscape and a mix of plant and animal life that's radically different from their pre–climate-change world.

One example of a species that may not adapt quickly enough to survive is the polar bear. These giant, iconic arctic animals, sometimes weighing 1,100 pounds (500 kg), are formidable carnivores. They have no natural predators. But they require an enormous amount of food. An adult polar bear burns more than 12,000 calories a day, even if the bear mainly spends its time lounging on the ice.

To take in enough calories, polar bears rely almost entirely on seal meat. More specifically, they rely on a very efficient seal-hunting method that biologists call still-hunting. Polar bears wait for hours beside seals' breathing holes in the sea ice. When a seal comes up for air, the bear smacks it on the head with both of its front paws to stun it, then bites it on the neck and drags it up onto the ice to eat. This hunting method requires sea ice. But climate change is warming the arctic. Higher temperatures mean earlier spring melts, later fall freezes, and less sea ice overall. With less ice, bears have to walk or swim long distances to find places to hunt, using calories and sapping their long-term health. As a result, most of the polar bear populations of the arctic are now in decline.

The effects of climate change can be seen by studying certain species, including the lionfish. Though the fish may thrive in warmer waters, their spread threatens the species upon which they feed.

Zebra-Striped Lionfish

Warmer temperatures are good for some species. But, as the case of the zebra-striped lionfish shows, one species' thriving can be catastrophic for other nearby organisms. The flashy, frilly-looking lionfish is native to the tropical areas of the Pacific Ocean, near the coasts of Australia, Malaysia, and Japan. They'd never been spotted in the Atlantic until the mid-1980s, when one was found off the coast of southern Florida.

The fish probably arrived in this new environment by way of aquariums. The fish were imported to the United States because their showy appearance was so appealing to home aquarium enthusiasts. Michelle Johnston, a biologist, explains what happened next. "Well, they like to eat. The lionfish start eating all the fish in the aquarium and people, instead of giving it back to the pet store, they just dump the fish." Released into the ocean, the lionfish do the same thing: eat lots of other fish. "They're the cockroaches of the sea," Johnston said.[50] One lionfish can eat up to 5,000 fish per year. And, in the right warm conditions, they reproduce quickly. In North American Atlantic waters, they have no natural predators. Their population has expanded along the coasts of Alabama, Louisiana, and Mississippi, as well as north along the Carolina coasts. The only thing that keeps them in check is cold water.

As the ocean warms due to climate change, lionfish will likely expand their range in the Atlantic. They are already having an impact on the diversity of marine life in the areas where they live. As climate conditions change, their effects may reach a much larger area and extend farther up the food chain. Florida research scientist Matthew Johnston says, "If left unchecked, there is the real potential that lionfish will have a negative impact on the fishing industry. It's likely that they are negatively impacting populations of the fish we like to eat, and at an alarming rate."[51]

Climate Change and Human Catastrophes

People often wonder whether specific hurricanes, floods, wildfires, or other catastrophes have been caused by climate change. Based on what scientists know so far, it's not possible to blame a specific event solely on the warming climate. But climate scientists are working on figuring out how much climate change increases the likelihood or intensity of certain catastrophes.

For instance, in 2017 two groups of scientists did detailed studies of Hurricane Harvey's record-breaking rainfall. They put data about the storm into two different computer models. One model represented real current conditions, where carbon dioxide levels have warmed the environment. The other model represented a world where the climate remains the same as it was 100 years ago, without carbon dioxide emissions. They compared the outcomes of the two models to make inferences about the impact of climate change.

They concluded that Harvey's rainfall over Texas was 15 to 38 percent higher than would be expected in a world without climate change. One of the studies, led by Geert Jan van Oldenborgh of the Royal Netherlands Meteorological Institute, also concluded that climate change increased the overall likelihood of a storm as strong as Harvey. Oldenborgh said, "The probability of such an event has increased by roughly a factor of three."[52] In other words, a storm with Harvey's strength might have happened without climate change. But, without climate change, it would only be expected to happen once every 3,000 years. With climate change, the likelihood is closer to once every 1,000 years.

This type of study is called an attribution study. Scientific studies often take many months or years to complete. But, over the past several years, Oldenborgh and other scientists have worked hard to do attribution studies quickly after major weather events. They do this in part because when weather catastrophes strike, many people jump to conclusions about whether climate change is or isn't to blame. "It's worthwhile to give the best scientific evidence at the time," Friederike Otto, another attribution researcher, said, "rather than not saying anything and letting others say things that are not related to what really happened."[53]

Hotter, dryer weather can lead to devastating wildfires. Many such fires have struck California in the first two decades of the twenty-first century.

Some types of events are easier to connect to climate change than others. Heat waves, periods of extreme cold, droughts, and extreme rainfall events are among the easiest. That's because scientists have a strong understanding of the basic processes that lead to those events. Wildfires, such as those in Indonesia, and tornadoes are much harder to attribute specifically to climate change. The processes that create those disasters are more complex and harder to model, and scientists don't have as strong an understanding of how warmer global temperatures may influence them.

Still, climate scientists have done strong attribution studies of many recent catastrophes, often finding that climate change was a significant factor. They've found climate change to be a factor in 2013 heat waves in Argentina and Europe, an extreme 2014 rainstorm in

France, an unusually hot spring in Korea in 2014, and the worldwide record-breaking temperatures in 2016, among many others.

Scientists are also investigating how climate change may create catastrophes that are less obviously weather-related. Some think that climate change may affect the spread of Ebola. Ebola outbreaks begin when humans are in close contact with infected wildlife. Anything that brings people and infected wildlife closer together may increase the risk of an outbreak. Climate change could cause animals to move to different habitats closer to humans. If droughts cause crop failures and food shortages, people may hunt more wildlife—including infected bats—creating more possibilities for human infection.

Human Catastrophes Ahead

Teams of climate scientists and others with expertise in understanding how catastrophes happen have used the available evidence to try to predict and prepare for the disasters that climate change may cause. The latest predictions are dire. Scientists anticipate that, if carbon emissions don't change course soon, a wide range of interconnected catastrophes will take place as the twenty-first century unfolds.

A major climate report issued by the US government in November 2018 says, "The assumption that current and future climate conditions will resemble the recent past is no longer valid."[54] The report says that some of the climate-related catastrophes that have already happened in the twenty-first century may be signs of what's coming next for the United States. Scientists think that extreme weather events similar to hurricanes Irma and Harvey will continue to damage infrastructure and interrupt trade, causing stress on the US economy. They expect that heat waves and high temperatures will lead to heat-related deaths and disease outbreaks. They say flooding will increase and droughts and fires will worsen and affect new areas. Due to droughts and hot weather, farms in the Midwest won't be able to produce as much food. The combined effects of these and other catastrophes could cause the US economy to shrink by up to 10 percent.

Another major climate report, released by the UN climate change panel in October 2018, predicts similar catastrophes worldwide. Written by ninety-one scientists from forty countries, it analyzes more than 6,000 climate studies. It predicts that catastrophic consequences for humans and the environment may take place as early as 2040. It says that, by 2040, the world may see increased wildfires and food shortages, widespread loss of coral reefs, droughts, and increased poverty. More than 50 million people in the United States, Bangladesh, China, Egypt, India, Indonesia, Japan, the Philippines, and Vietnam will be vulnerable to increased flooding due to higher sea levels.

The UN report goes further to predict what might happen if global temperatures rise even higher than that expected 2040 level. One possibility: due to heat making areas uninhabitable, there will be massive movements of people out of heat-burdened areas in search of livable land. Such migrations could make the Rohingya exodus of 700,000 people look minor. With such waves of migration, international borders may become irrelevant in some areas. Aromar Revi, one of the authors of the report, said, "You can set up a wall to try to contain 10,000 and 20,000 and one million people, but not 10 million."[55]

> **"The assumption that current and future climate conditions will resemble the recent past is no longer valid."[54]**
>
> —2018 US National Climate Assessment

> **"You can set up a wall to try to contain 10,000 and 20,000 and one million people, but not 10 million."[55]**
>
> *—Aromar Revi, Director of the Indian Institute for Human Settlements, on why extreme heat and mass migrations may make some international borders irrelevant*

Responses to Climate Change

The evidence overwhelmingly shows that human-driven climate change is happening and will likely cause catastrophes in the near future. But some people say that climate change is not real or that climate change is a natural process, not caused by humans. There is not good evidence to back up these statements. But the people who make them are sometimes very powerful, which influences others' impressions of the issue.

For example, the United States is the world's largest economy and the world's second-largest producer of greenhouse gases. In November 2018, thirteen US government agencies released a 1,656-page report based on decades of climate research by hundreds of scientists. The report predicted dramatic effects on every part of the country and the economy and called for quick action to reduce greenhouse gas emissions.

President Donald Trump responded to the climate change report, saying, "I don't believe it," without giving any evidence to back up his disbelief.[56] He also contended, "You have scientists on both sides of the picture."[57] In fact, six independent studies of scientific consensus on this subject have found that there is not significant division among scientists about this issue. Over 97 percent of active climate scientists share the understanding, from all the evidence, that climate change exists, is human-driven, and is a significant and growing danger. Statements such as Trump's are not based on evidence. They spread the false impression that climate change is poorly understood.

This makes it harder to fix the problems climate change is already causing and harder to avoid future catastrophes.

Many world leaders take climate change seriously. In 2015, 195 countries signed on to what became known as the Paris climate agreement. The agreement requires each country to take action

Youth Sue the US Government over Climate Change

The twenty-one young people who initiated the lawsuit *Juliana v. United States* say the US government has violated their rights by failing to address climate change. They want the court to order the government to take action to lower the carbon dioxide levels in the atmosphere and stop the trend of global warming.

The government has pushed back against the suit, making many appeals to prevent the case from going to trial. It has argued that the lawsuit is an "improper" attempt to have the courts intervene in policy decisions. It also says that the youth haven't shown that the government has harmed them in a concrete way. And it has argued that it's not possible to link specific harms to climate change.

US District Judge Ann Aiken, who has heard arguments in the case, said, "Exercising my 'reasoned judgment,' I have no doubt that the right to a climate system capable of sustaining human life is fundamental to a free and ordered society." Lawyers say that even if the youth win this case, it's likely to be appealed in a higher court and possibly even in the Supreme Court.

The group first filed the suit in Oregon in 2015. A trial date was set and postponed several times over the course of 2018. If the suit does go to trial, each of the twenty-one plaintiffs, ages eleven through twenty-two, will testify about the specific harms they claim the government's actions have caused them.

Quoted in "Juliana v. US Climate Lawsuit." Our Children's Trust, n.d., www.ourchildrenstrust.org.

toward reducing carbon emissions. Michael Levi, an energy and climate change policy expert, described the agreement's importance. He said, "The world finally has a framework for cooperating on climate change that's suited to the task. Whether or not this becomes a true turning point for the world, though, depends critically on how seriously countries follow through."[58]

In 2017, Trump announced that the United States would no longer participate in the Paris agreement. But a group of twenty US states and more than fifty major US cities pledged to meet their commitments under the agreement even if the country as a whole withdraws. And other nations, including China and the countries of the European Union, have put programs in place to reduce carbon emissions.

Climate Change and Catastrophes in the Twenty-First Century

Climate change, so far, is the defining worldwide catastrophe of the twenty-first century. It's a human-generated shift that magnifies natural disasters and has the potential to affect every being on Earth. Several of the landmark disasters of this century's first decades—record-breaking hurricanes Harvey and Irma and Indonesia's mega fires—can be seen as signs of what's to come if we continue the activities that are driving climate change.

Some sources of sudden tragedy cannot be eliminated. There's no way to control earthquakes. Ebola and other similar viruses will likely always exist in some form. Some number of extreme storms, floods, and fires, will still happen, even if we bring global warming under control. But, in many cases, it's possible to limit the amount of suffering that these disasters cause. In a world with growing inequality

Finding alternate, cleaner sources of energy is one way humanity can slow down and even reverse the process of climate change. This could potentially save lives in the future by making catastrophes less severe.

between the rich and the poor, alleviating poverty may be one of the most helpful responses to catastrophes of all kinds.

And some catastrophes can be prevented. People have a great deal of control over how we generate energy to power our societies, how we handle waste and hazardous materials, how we treat one another, and how we take care of important resources. We can use the catastrophes of the first part of the twenty-first century as warning signs. By looking at the facts about past and current disasters, understanding their causes, and drawing on the resilience and compassion of those who have survived catastrophes already, we can avoid a great deal of suffering in the rest of the century.

SOURCE NOTES

Introduction: Rising Waters in Houston

1. Erik S. Blake and David A. Zelinsky, "National Hurricane Center Tropical Cyclone Report: Hurricane Harvey," *NOAA*, May 9, 2018. http://nhc.noaa.gov.

2. Quoted in Julie Turkewitz, Manny Fernandez, and Alan Blinder, "In Houston, Anxiety and Frantic Rescues as Floodwaters Rise," *New York Times*, August 27, 2018. www.nytimes.com.

3. Quoted in Oliver Milman, "'Your Eyes Start Itching': Pollution Soars in Houston After Chemical Industry Leaks," *Guardian*, September 2, 2017. www.theguardian.com.

4. Quoted in Elaina Plott, "Hurricane Harvey Is Houston's Unending Nightmare," *Atlantic*, August 26, 2018. www.theatlantic.com.

5. Quoted in Manny Fernandez, "A Year After Hurricane Harvey, Houston's Poorest Neighborhoods Are Slowest to Recover," *New York Times*, September 3, 2018. www.nytimes.com.

6. Quoted in Fernandez, "A Year After Hurricane Harvey."

Chapter 1: How Have Natural Disasters Affected the Planet?

7. Quoted in Megan Rowling, "Natural Disasters Cause Way More Deaths in Poor Countries Than Rich Ones," *Huffington Post*, October 13, 2016. www.huffingtonpost.com.

8. Quoted in James Sturcke, "Haiti Earthquake: Survivors' Stories," *Guardian*, January 14, 2010. www.theguardian.com.

9. Quoted in "Haiti: The Shattered Year," *New York Times*, 2018. www.nytimes.com.

10. Quoted in "Haiti: The Shattered Year."

11. Quoted in Martin Fackler, "Powerful Quake and Tsunami Devastate Northern Japan," *New York Times*, March 11, 2011. www.nytimes.com.

12. Quoted in Fackler, "Powerful Quake and Tsunami Devastate Northern Japan."

13. Quoted in Martin Fackler, "Japanese Coastal Town Still Struggling to Rebuild from 2011 Tsunami," *New York Times*, March 12, 2015. www.nytimes.com.

14. Quoted in Aryn Baker, "One Man's Story of Surviving Ebola," *Time*, October 2, 2014. www.time.com.

15. Rebecca Johnson, "Ebola Survivor: 'Demonic' Disease 'Worse Than War,'" *CNN*, February 6, 2015. www.cnn.com.

16. Quoted in Didrik Schanche and Sami Yenigun, "Ebola Survivor: 'You Feel Like . . . Maybe . . . A Ghost,'" *NPR*, December 25, 2014. www.npr.org.

17. Quoted in Oliver Milman, "From Harvey to Michael: How America's Year of Major Hurricanes Unfolded," *Guardian*, October 16, 2018. www.theguardian.com.

18. Quoted in "In the Eye of the Caribbean Storm: One Year On from Maria and Irma," *UN News*, September 5, 2018. http://news.un.org.

19. Quoted in "In the Eye of the Caribbean Storm."

20. Quoted in "In the Eye of the Caribbean Storm."

21. Quoted in Milman, "From Harvey to Michael."

Chapter 2: How Have Catastrophes in Nature Affected the Planet?

22. Quoted in David Barstow, David Rohde, and Stephanie Saul, "Deepwater Horizon's Final Hours," *New York Times*, December 25, 2010. www.nytimes.com.

23. Quoted in Barstow, "Deepwater Horizon's Final Hours."

24. Quoted in Barstow, "Deepwater Horizon's Final Hours."

25. Quoted in Oliver Milman, "Deepwater Horizon Disaster Altered Building Blocks of Ocean Life," *Guardian*, June 28, 2018. www.theguardian.com.

26. Quoted in Carl Hoffmann, "Special Report: Why the BP Oil Rig Blowout Happened," *Popular Mechanics*, September 2, 2010. www.popularmechanics.com.

27. "Interior Department Releases Final Well Control Regulations to Ensure Safe and Responsible Offshore Oil and Gas Development," *US Department of the Interior*, April 14, 2016. www.doi.gov.

28. Quoted in Angel L. Martinez Cantera, "Indonesia's Forest Fires Threaten Sumatra's Few Remaining Orang Rimba," *Guardian*, June 7, 2016. www.theguardian.com.

29. Quoted in John Vidal, "Indonesia's Forest Fires Threaten a Third of World's Wild Orangutans," *Guardian*, October 26, 2015. www.theguardian.com.

30. Quoted in "Great Pacific Garbage Patch," *National Geographic*, September 19, 2014. www.nationalgeographic.com.

31. Quoted in Livia Albeck-Ripka, "The 'Great Pacific Garbage Patch' Is Ballooning, 87,000 Tons of Plastic and Counting," *New York Times*, March 22, 2018. www.nytimes.com.

32. Quoted in Doyle Rice, "World's Largest Collection of Ocean Garbage Is Twice the Size of Texas," *USA Today*, March 22, 2018. www.usatoday.com.

33. Laura Parker, "Floating Trash Collector Set to Tackle Pacific Garbage Patch," *National Geographic*, September 7, 2018. www.nationalgeographic.com.

Chapter 3: How Have Human Catastrophes Affected the Planet?

34. Quoted in Anna Clark, "'Nothing to Worry About. The Water Is Fine.': How Flint Poisoned Its People," *Guardian*, July 3, 2018. www.theguardian.com.

35. Quoted in Clark, "Nothing to Worry About."

36. Merrit Kennedy, "Independent Investigators: State Officials Mostly to Blame for Flint Water Crisis," *NPR*, March 23, 2016. www.npr.org.

37. Quoted in Ari Shapiro, "What's Changed and What Hasn't When It Comes to the Flint Water Crisis," *NPR*, October 26, 2018. www.npr.org.

38. Quoted in Shapiro, "What's Changed and What Hasn't."

39. Quoted in Michael Safi, "'Tied to Trees and Raped': UN Report Details Rohingya Horrors," *Guardian*, September 18, 2018. www.theguardian.com.

40. Quoted in "AP Finds Mass Graves, Latest Evidence of Rohingya Genocide in Myanmar," *CBS News*, February 1, 2018. www.cbsnews.com.

41. Quoted in Krishnadev Calamur, "The Misunderstood Roots of Burma's Rohingya Crisis," *Atlantic*, September 25, 2017. www.theatlantic.com.

42. Quoted in Hannah Beech, "'No Such Thing as Rohingya': Myanmar Erases a History," *New York Times*, December 2, 2017. www.nytimes.com.

43. Quoted in "Rohingya Genocide Is Still Going On, Says Top UN Investigator," *Guardian*, October 24, 2018. www.theguardian.com.

44. Quoted in Ed Yong, "What Was Lost in Brazil's Devastating Museum Fire," *Atlantic*, September 4, 2018. www.theatlantic.com.

45. Quoted in Michael Greshko, "Fire Devastates Brazil's Oldest Science Museum," *National Geographic*, September 6, 2018. www.nationalgeographic.com.

46. Quoted in Greshko, "Fire Devastates Brazil's Oldest Science Museum."

47. Quoted in Greshko, "Fire Devastates Brazil's Oldest Science Museum."

48. Quoted in Gabriella Angeleti, "'Brazil's Donald Trump' Jair Bolsonaro May Thwart Efforts to Rebuild Rio Museum Destroyed in Fire," *Art Newspaper*, October 29, 2018. www.theartnewspaper.com.

Chapter 4: How Has Climate Change Affected the Planet?

49. "Scientific Consensus: Earth's Climate Is Warming," *NASA*, n.d., http://climate.nasa.gov.

50. Quoted in Alex Stuckey, "Lionfish Invasion in the Gulf of Mexico Expected to Worsen as the Climate Changes," *Houston Chronicle*, November 14, 2018. www.houstonchronicle.com.

51. Quoted in Stuckey, "Lionfish Invasion in the Gulf of Mexico."

52. Quoted in Harry Fountain, "Scientists Link Hurricane Harvey's Record Rainfall to Climate Change," *New York Times*, December 13, 2017. www.nytimes.com.

53. Quoted in Harry Fountain, "Looking, Quickly, for the Fingerprints of Climate Change," *New York Times*, August 1, 2017. www.nytimes.com.

54. Quoted in Coral Davenport and Kendra Pierre-Louis, "US Climate Report Warns of Damaged Environment and Shrinking Economy," *New York Times*, November 23, 2018. www.nytimes.com.

55. Quoted in Coral Davenport, "Major Climate Report Describes a Strong Risk of Crisis as Early as 2040," *New York Times*, October 7, 2018. www.nytimes.com.

56. Quoted in Chris Cillizza, "Donald Trump Buried a Climate Change Report Because 'I Don't Believe It,'" *CNN*, November 27, 2018. www.cnn.com.

57. Quoted in William Cummings, "'I Have a Natural Instinct for Science,' President Trump Says in Newly Released Interview," *USA Today*, October 17, 2018. www.usatoday.com.

58. Quoted in Coral Davenport, "Nations Approve Landmark Climate Accord in Paris," *New York Times*, December 12, 2015. www.nytimes.com.

FOR FURTHER RESEARCH

Books

Connie Goldsmith, *The Ebola Epidemic: The Fight, The Future*. Minneapolis, MN: Twenty-First Century Books, 2016.

Andrea C. Nakaya, *What Are the Consequences of Climate Change?* San Diego, CA: ReferencePoint Press, 2017.

Cliff Waterford, *Hurricane Harvey*. Minneapolis, MN: Abdo Publishing, 2018.

Christine Wilcox, *Careers in Emergency Response*. San Diego, CA: ReferencePoint Press, 2017.

Edward Willett, *Hurricane Irma*. Minneapolis, MN: Abdo Publishing, 2018.

Internet Sources

"Environmental Health Student Portal," *National Library of Medicine*, n.d., http://kidsenvirohealth.nlm.nih.gov.

Ruth Tam. "This Is How You Get Ebola," *PBS*, August 21, 2014. www.pbs.org.

"Visualizing How Ocean Currents Help Create the Garbage Patches," *NOAA*, 2018. http://response.restoration.noaa.gov.

Websites

Fourth National US Climate Assessment

http://nca2018.globalchange.gov

The 2018 government report on the current and predicted state of climate change in the United States includes interactive graphics and information on current and expected future impacts and suggested solutions.

NASA's Global Climate Change / Vital Signs of the Planet

http://climate.nasa.gov

NASA's website features scientifically backed information on the evidence, causes, and effects of global, human-driven climate change.

National Hurricane Center

www.nhc.noaa.gov

On the website of the National Hurricane Center, users can track current Atlantic and Pacific storms and learn about past cyclones and hurricanes.

United Nations High Commissioner for Refugees

www.unhcr.org/en-us

The UN website includes up-to-date stories on the Rohingya crisis and other refugee crises.

INDEX

INDEX CONTINUED

IMAGE CREDITS

ABOUT THE AUTHOR

Carolyn Williams-Noren writes poems and lyric essays in addition to nonfiction for young readers. She lives in Minneapolis with her husband and two daughters.